MAD

MAD

SEEING YOUR ANGER WITH THE CLARITY OF GOD'S WORD

RICK THOMAS

MAD:
Seeing Your Anger with the Clarity of God's Word

ISBN 978-1-7323854-4-3

Rick Thomas

© 2025 Life Over Coffee

Unless otherwise noted, all Scripture references herein are from the English Standard Version, copyright © 2001 by Crossway, Inc. Used by permission. All rights reserved.

No part of this publication may be reproduced, stored in a retrieval system, or transmitted in any form or by any means without the express written permission of Life Over Coffee.

Edited by Sarah Hayhurst

Life Over Coffee
8595 Pelham Rd Ste 400 #406,
Greenville, SC 29615
LifeOverCoffee.com

Dedication

Dave, Lorra Beth, David, Mary, Kevin, Deborah, Will, and Kathy

Thank you for your care, provision, encouragement, and faith in the Lord's good work through this ministry. We exist in no small measure because of you.

Know this, my beloved brothers: let every person be quick to hear, slow to speak, slow to anger; for the anger of man does not produce the righteousness of God. Therefore put away all filthiness and rampant wickedness and receive with meekness the implanted word, which is able to save your souls. But be doers of the word, and not hearers only, deceiving yourselves.

(James 1:19–22)

For additional resources, visit

lifeovercoffee.com

Table of Contents

   Preface 10
   Introduction.. 14
1 Righteous Anger... 22
2 Diagramming Anger 30
3 Silent Treatment 42
4 Seeing Clearly 48
5 Angry Puppets 58
6 The God Quest.. 66
7 Helping the Angry 76
   Conclusion... 84
   About the Author.. 90

Preface

Anger is our most common temptation. When we take in the full breadth of the manifestations of anger, it makes sense because we know about our struggle with anger, and we've seen it too many times in others. The parent who expels air in frustration over the child who placed that final straw on the camel's back because of the child's multiple blunders throughout the day is expressing anger. The friend who rolls their eyes self-righteously looks down on someone, expressing anger. The preacher who hears one more complaint from a church member will say nothing to the grumbler but "murders" them in his heart, an unguarded habituation in sinful anger. Then there are our marriages, the most well-worn battleground where all our skirmishes are always in view. Marriage is an unbreakable covenant where our strengths and weaknesses become the opportunity to put on Christ or respond with our preferred anger iteration.

In this book, I'm addressing our most common foe and the battleground of our hearts where anger finds its power. I hope you will do as I have done by making this book a devotional that points to you rather than thinking about how much someone else needs to read these things. Perhaps you're right; they must know what's between these covers. After you digest it and do the hard, soul-searching work of identifying and disassembling your idols, you will be in the proper humble posture to give them a copy. How marvelous would it be for a friend to care so much to provide them with medicine for their souls! But first, will you follow my lead? This book is for all of us, and we want to be our first counselee. So sit back. Read expectantly. Ask the Spirit of God to illuminate those places that require such light, and beg Him to break into any complex and crusty places.

> Batter my heart, three-person'd God, for you
> As yet but knock, breathe, shine, and seek to mend;
> That I may rise and stand, o'erthrow me, and bend
> Your force to break, blow, burn, and make me new.
> John Donne

Unless I say otherwise, all references in this book to anger speak of sinful, unrighteous anger. I say this to thwart any impulse for someone to say, "Hey, what about righteous anger?" However, because there can be a reflexive response that blows past sinful anger because we want to label it as righteous, I will begin this book talking about righteous anger to know how to distinguish between the excellent and evil types of anger. It won't hurt to rethink and re-examine how we view our righteous anger. As I have re-examined my anger, there have been times when I realized it was not as righteous as I had hoped. How did I know this? I asked the recipients of my anger, which nearly always was a family member. Though I did not see what I said as sinful, the way it landed on them told another story. The righteous anger of Jesus was not like mine. Perhaps you may find an opportunity to rethink and recalibrate your anger.

I am grateful you're reading this book. My one appeal is that you treat it not as your typical book. Let me modify what I mean. Like my other books, this one is a workbook. Most people who read books place them in short-term memory while highlighting a few helpful quotes. This book will be just like that if you read without stopping, reflecting, reacting, and possibly repenting. I have added calls to action at the end of each chapter. I don't want my readers just to read, but I want them to "work out their salvation with fear and trembling" (Philippians 2:13) as they go through each chapter. Perhaps you will need to sit and soak in a chapter for a day or two. Maybe you want to throw in a writing assignment or talk to a close friend—the more, the merrier. This book will work with you proportionally to the work you put into it. And if you have anger problems, you will experience remarkable change by the end—if you do the work.

Thank you for reading. Enjoy the ride. I am very grateful you would take the time for such a vital endeavor.

Rick

Preface

Introduction

> What causes quarrels and what causes fights among you? Is it not this, that your passions are at war within you? You desire and do not have, so you murder. You covet and cannot obtain, so you fight and quarrel.
> (James 4:1–2)

Anger is consistently minimized, even among Christians, especially among Christians. The unwitting temptation is to reclassify our anger to lesser-sounding offenses. When I talk to people about being angry, the response usually follows, "Oh no, I'm not an angry person. I think if I were angry, I would respond differently than this. I'm just frustrated." They believe my anger diagnosis is wrong when the person I'm talking to has softened their language to the point where their conscience no longer perceives their sinful anger. Their "internal moral thermostat" has learned to keep quiet because the person is deeply habituated to these types of rationalizations. What they don't recognize is that frustration is a euphemism for anger. This graphic illustrates several forms of sinful anger, though it only partially lists anger terms. (I'll explain the graphic in a moment.)

Maybe a few of your oft-used ones are not represented on this graphic. For a double bonus, it would be an excellent leadership opportunity to show this graphic to your family or a few close friends to gain their perspective on how they experience you.

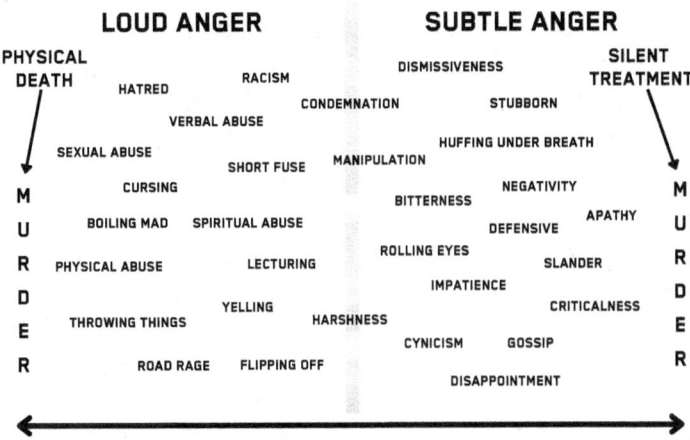

THE ANGER SPECTRUM
MANY MANIFESTATIONS OF ONE SIN

As the graphic shows, our anger manifests itself on a spectrum. Everyone has their preferred way of getting angry, so our labels must be clear when discussing the darker side of our communication patterns. Without understanding the gradations of our anger, we will not perceive what we're doing to others, which means we cannot change. Do you remember what Paul said? We are to do away with our former manner of life, but here is the problem: if we do not know how to put off those bad habits because of inaccurate assessments, our destructive behaviors will not change (Ephesians 4:22). Thus, we want to be vigilant about taking our souls to task to see if there is any iniquity in us regarding how we speak to others.

Little Nails Are Big

If you see the graphic as a giant bucket encompassing many forms of anger, you understand the point correctly. The manifestations and euphemisms have one big label slapped on the side of the bucket; it's anger. Like there are shades of black, there are shades of anger. Now, I'm not the "word police," and if you want to call your anger by a euphemism, that is fine with me as long as you're willing to acknowledge it is wrong. I realize the consequences of anger are different. Still, any sin we commit makes us guilty of them all (James 2:10). Just because we're not the kind of people to throw a chair across a room or yell obscenities in congested traffic, it does not mean we may use a smaller nail to put Christ on the cross to feel better about ourselves. He died for all our sins, not just the big ones. Regrettably, this book does not address all the consequences of anger but sticks to one point: how to recognize and repent of anger regardless of the manifestation. The upside is that if we can root out all traces of this ubiquitous enemy, whatever consequential effects we have on others will mitigate mightily.

Perhaps you express anger through impatience, apathy, dismissiveness, or frustration. Most of us have "refined" our anger manifestations to the subtle side of the Anger Spectrum. I have. Impatience is my number one anger sin. I like to get things done; I've always been this way, but how unfair would it be to map my strength, skill, or habits over others who are not like me? I must not do that. I have to work on myself uniquely, never minimizing, but hopefully ridding myself of this sin, which is why I'm writing this book. You're probably like me, where the more coarse and obvious anger sins do not typically characterize civilized believers. Of course, the downside is how the temptation to tamp down and accept our actions is all the more vital. Being blind to our blindness is the worst possible condition of the soul, so we must be honest with how we see ourselves. But if that is a challenge due to any hardening of our consciences, perhaps studying these verses will soften things up. See Hebrews 3:7-8, 4:7, and 5:12-14.

Comparison Trap

> Not that we dare to classify or compare ourselves with some of those who are commending themselves. But when they measure themselves by one another and compare themselves with one another, they are without understanding.
>
> (2 Corinthians 10:12)

Then there is the comparison trap. Whenever we sense the urge to compare ourselves with others, the best course of action is to compare ourselves to Christ. It's easy to compare ourselves to the fifth graders, but where does that leave us? We may feel better about ourselves, but there is no motivation to change. Anyone serious about transformation looks to people farther along with goals they have not attained. The comparison trap is a snare that will give us a sense of accomplishment and even justification for our anger. Once we remove the grievousness of our sin by rounding off the jagged edges, there will be less motivation to change.

The wise person will let Christ be the measuring stick that gauges their maturity. Though comparing ourselves with others can make us feel better about ourselves, comparing ourselves to Christ is a more honest reality check. One of the ways we can do this is by filtering our anger through the interpretive grid James uses in James 4:1-2. If the anger manifestation is sinful, then we're talking murder. Perhaps this label is striking to you; it was when I first thought seriously about what he was saying. But if you peel the label anger from the bucket of manifestations and slap a new one on it, a murderous one, it might be a game-changer, as it was for me.

Anger Spectrum

Look at my Anger Spectrum; you will see the word murder at each end. On the far left is physical murder, which says, "I do not want you to exist any longer," and on the other end is the silent treatment, which says, "I can't kill you because I'm a nice person, but I can treat you as though you don't exist any longer." Physical murder is a consequentially worse manifestation of anger, but this book is not dealing with the all-important subject of consequences. The point here is that any form of anger is an offense against a holy God who refuses to listen to the petty manipulations of our rationalizations. My strongest appeal is for us not to succumb to the "consequential argument" as a way to wiggle from the repentance that should be forthcoming when there are lesser degrees of anger burying itself into the dark places of our hearts.

Murder is one of the ways we communicate the sin of anger in our home; it helps our family to level the playing field and aggressively engage any heart going wayward. Though we don't want to give ourselves over to non-redemptive hyperbole because the label murder could sound that way, we hope to see the seriousness and wretchedness of our anger. We must take all sin seriously because any evil—big and small—puts Christ on the cross. When I am impatient, I have found it helpful to think of myself as a murderer. When I see myself as a murderer, there is no place to run, hide, or fight. There is only one option: repent to God and those who experienced my specific version of anger.

Name It, Claim It

- Do you want wiggle room when it comes to your anger?
- Do you want to skirt around your anger, no matter how small it may appear?
- Isn't it better to steer away from ambiguous and subjective gradations?

> ... to put off your old self, which belongs to your former manner of life and is corrupt through deceitful desires, and to be renewed in the spirit of your minds, and to put on the new self, created after the likeness of God in true righteousness and holiness.
>
> (Ephesians 4:22–24)

If you're serious about change, give anger the full credit it deserves. Name it and claim it. Rather than lounging around the pool of purposeless excuses and ceaseless misdirections, jump into the water of God's cleansing Word (Ephesians 5:26) and be brutally honest with yourself. Once you've identified what you need to put off, you can move to the transformative stages of renewing your mind and putting on a new kind of person that is created differently from you, from all of us (Ephesians 5:1). That mindset is humility, which is the one condition that opens the door to God's empowering favor on our lives (James 4:6).

Call to Action

You're reading a book on anger. It addresses our universal problem with this sin from many different angles. It will help anyone who wants to change. More than likely, you have not physically murdered anyone, but you, like me, have murdered in other ways. Will you take the time to wrestle through this Introduction by answering these questions? There is no hurry. The time invested will be worth the result that could be yours. And if you struggle with anger, your relationships, especially your closest ones, will be forever grateful for the effort you put forth here.

1. Will you acknowledge your anger, regardless of the type? Which one is your most-oft expression? Will you write it down and then add a short prayer, pleading with the Lord to change you?
2. Will you see how your anger is a sin that motivated the Father to crush His Son (Isaiah 53:10) on a cross so you could experience His salvation? Reflect on that thought for a moment. Will you share with a friend what you're thinking, how you want to change, and your gratitude for God's transformational power?
3. Once a person gets past the things they do to water down, hide behind, or make excuses for their anger, they'll be able to find the restoration the Father freely provides to humble souls. Rather than guarding our reputations, our best call to action is to ask the Spirit of God to illuminate our minds. Will you ask Him as you move through this book?

Introduction

1

Righteous Anger

Before I delve into a deeper analysis of anger and how to overcome it, there is another kind that is not sinful. We call it righteous anger. It will be helpful if we spend some time thinking about what it is and is not because there are times when a person's anger is righteous. It is always wise and humble to be careful about how we think about our anger rather than impulsively slapping the righteous label on it. However, it might be the case in a few isolated situations. You can be angry and sin not. The problem is that there are times when it's hard to tell if a person's anger is righteous, so I want to examine it before we get into our more common foe—sinful anger. One of the complicating problems about righteous anger is that most of us have a high view of ourselves—at least a little bit. Thinking highly of ourselves creates a faulty interpretative filter, which will tempt us to color our anger righteously, something I've done more than once. I'm sure you've been there too. The temptation to reclassify our angry sin events is alluring.

Distinguish the Difference

Righteous anger is the term we use to describe someone who is not sinning when angry, but the question is, how do you know if your anger is righteous or unrighteous? What does righteous anger do that sinful anger cannot? Ephesians 4:26, James 1:20, and Matthew 21:12-14 are three popular texts validating righteous anger. Of course, the Psalms are full of passages where people express anger to God regarding the evil in our world. There are also the Proverbs, where we learn about sinful anger. I do not struggle with putting all these verses together—or at least some of them—and placing them under righteous anger.

My concern is that some people are too quick to label their anger as righteous, while those on the receiving end of their anger are more hurt than helped by it, which is a vital key when determining the righteousness of one's anger—its effect on others. The redemptive purpose of anger implies that righteous anger has elements that do not comprise sinful anger. Because we tend to esteem ourselves more than others, wise individuals desire a solid, biblical footing for their beliefs and practices. Let's look at three identifying elements in this chapter and compare your most recent anger display with them. Think about the last time you were angry at someone. Before reading further, how would you classify it as righteous or unrighteous? Maybe you can reflect on when you were confident your anger was righteous. With your illustration in mind, how does it compare with the following three-point analysis?

Anger and Humility

Discerning our anger is essential, especially if we have been sinfully angry, which I'm calling unrighteous. We must identify any sin in our anger regardless of how we categorize it. (See the Anger Spectrum in the Introduction to refamiliarize yourself with some of the many manifestations of anger.) Suppose we do not perceive sin in our anger, even though it's there. If so, we will not seek to repent, a process that begins with putting the bad behavior off while linking to renewing our minds and wrapping up with putting on a new person that resembles Jesus. Thus, the best starting point to discern between righteous and unrighteous anger is a healthy dose of self-suspicion, which will aid in this deeper analysis. I have already referred to our "high view of ourselves," which makes self-suspicion an essential ingredient in our sanctification, whether discussing anger or any other bad habit.

If you are a Christian, you should have enough biblical common sense to know how quickly we can deceive ourselves. Unfortunately, if you are anything like me, you will not have all the clarity you need to perceive the traces of sin in your anger, primarily when you direct it toward others. With a healthy dose of self-suspicion as our starting point, we want to ask our friends their perspectives, assuming they have observed our anger and sense the freedom to speak into our lives. If it's a family member you're asking, you have an excellent leadership opportunity before you, hoping to unify any fractures in the family. Of course, if your anger is truly righteous, you are humble enough—another righteous quality—to ask others how they experience you. If you're unwilling to ask someone to analyze your anger, you probably have your answer.

- Do you have a healthy dose of self-suspicion about how you observe yourself? What does this mean? How does this awareness play out practically in your life?
- Do you regularly ask others how they experience your communication? If not, why not? We can do many things alone, but sanctification is not one of them.

Anger and Redemption

And Jesus entered the temple and drove out all who sold and bought in the temple, and he overturned the tables of the money-changers and the seats of those who sold pigeons. He said to them, "It is

> written, 'My house shall be called a house of prayer,' but you make it a den of robbers." And the blind and the lame came to him in the temple, and he healed them.
> (Matthew 21:12-14)

The most famous passage used when discussing righteous anger is when Jesus turned the tables over in the temple. I will use this one for our analysis of righteous anger. This passage is essential for any discussion on anger, but it is even more so when discerning the differences between righteous and unrighteous communication. This portion of Scripture is narrative; it is telling a story. The point of the passage is not about anger or how to diagnose your anger, though there are some things we can learn about the anger of Jesus, one of which is the redemptive nature of His anger, a key aspect. Though He physically harmed a few tables, He did not physically harm any humans. The point of His anger was not to be verbally abusive toward anyone but restorative in the lives of those who would listen to Him. The result of His anger aligns with what Paul taught about our communication style in Ephesians—to build up another person.

> Let no corrupting talk come out of your mouths, but only such as is good for building up, as fits the occasion, that it may give grace to those who hear.
> (Ephesians 4:29)

Some people in the temple that day were sabotaging the temple's purposes, which is the point of the passage. Jesus wanted them to know how they had defiled the temple and how He would not stand for it. His desire was not to hurt anyone but to draw attention to the unrighteous error some were making. He wanted to redeem their religion by presenting the right one, not harming humans. Perhaps reflecting on these questions will aid you in examining your anger responses.

- Is your anger restorative in that you are drawing attention to unrighteous errors? This question is about your patterns of anger, not necessarily episodic moments. We all flub up, but how folks would characterize you is in view here.
- Is the primary motive for your anger about not defiling God's fame, or is your anger more about what you are not getting (James 4:1–3)?

Anger and Community

And the blind and the lame came to him in the temple, and he healed them.
(Matthew 21:14)

Another interesting observation about the anger of Jesus is that the folks who needed His restorative care were not afraid of Him. Though He hated the sinfulness He observed in the temple that day, those who needed and wanted His restorative care came to Him, seeking His tenderness and touch. You see it when Matthew talks about the blind and lame seeking the Savior. Righteous anger does not scare people away from the righteously angry person because they perceive the person's humility, genuineness, and ability to help them. Jesus was able to be angry and caring at the same time. He had power over His power: anger was His human power, but the Spirit's power over Him modulated His human power. One power will always rule, and the other will submit. Our anger won't be sinful when divine power overrides and superintends our human power.

Unrighteous anger is a different beast because its unleashing comes from rogue destructive human motives and deceptions. The anger of Jesus was Spirit-led and Spirit-managed. Spirit-controlled anger allowed Him to focus His fury on the sinfulness at hand. Unlike a raging river out of its banks, His anger did not negatively affect those who needed more than His righteous indignation. If our anger is righteous, it should not be a stumbling block to those within earshot to find help, even from the one expressing anger. Righteousness begets righteousness, not unrighteousness. Remember James 1:20?

- Do righteous purposes control your anger, or does it jump the banks and hurt those who need your care? (Again, I'm speaking of our patterns or habits of anger, not necessarily an episode. How does your anger characterize you?)
- Does your anger inhibit people from engaging you for redemptive purposes? Are others afraid of you?

Call to Action

One of the keys to this chapter is humility. If you are humble, you want to share these ideas with those within your sphere of influence to examine any needed growth areas. If you're unwilling to share these things with a friend, you know where you are with your anger manifestations.

1. For the humble and courageous, would you work through all the questions I have already asked you in this chapter with someone close to you?
2. Do you ask others their opinion of your anger? If not, why not?
3. Are you the only person you allow to judge your anger? If so, why so?
4. Do your patterns of anger have redemptive (or restorative) purposes? Describe a time when it did and did not.
5. Does the Spirit of God control your anger? How do you know? How did your friend respond to this question?
6. When you are angry, do you sense the Spirit of God managing the force of your anger? Describe a moment like this and the outcome.

Righteous Anger

2

Diagramming Anger

Have you ever wondered what is going on in the mind of the angry person? It's not what you might think. Anger is our most common and problematic enemy that can set up camp in our hearts. If practiced often, it can become a habit that destroys our souls and relationships. Yes, our souls; it's more than a behavior. It's a heart condition, first of all. To get rid of it, we must understand its exact cause. We will take down the behavior as we address the source practically.

Anger Deceives

Anger is also one of our most accepted behavioral sin habits. Its subtle deception is the most dangerous aspect of anger. If everybody is doing it, then it is not a big deal. The sad thing about not recognizing our anger as a sin issue is that we cannot repent of something we accept, ignore, blame, or don't perceive (Hebrews 3:7-8, 4:7, and 5:12-14). The most common mistake when thinking about sinful anger is its subtleness. The word anger conjures big things like rage. You may remember Bobby Knight, the Indiana Hoosier basketball coach, throwing a chair across the gymnasium floor. Volatile anger is a problem; we're all familiar with road rage. Then there is hate speech, of course.

Anger is much more than these things. There is a more refined side to this hideous sin. I'm not suggesting they are the same consequentially, as addressed already. We all know that physical murder is far worse than silent treatment, and if we had the choice, everyone would pick "don't speak to me" over "don't kill me." But you can also make the case that any sin puts Christ on the cross, which is why we must talk about how the ubiquitous nature of anger is more subtle than overt, which is the danger. More people participate in these milder forms of murder, making them more destructive in everyday relationships.

Anger Illustrated

You desire and do not have, so you murder.
(James 4:2)

Some years ago, our daughter walked across the living room, away from her mother, while responding to her mother by huffing under her breath. Her response was a low grade on the Anger Spectrum. I stopped her to inquire about her sinful anger while offering her an opportunity to repent from her sin against God and my wife. She did, thankfully. James had a profound descriptor for what she did. He called it murder. Strikingly, James did not trim anger to its most innocuous form to feel better about our actions. He put sinful anger in one basket—a murderous one.

Suppose we reduced sin to acceptable behavior. In that case, we are well on our way to becoming okay with it while never recognizing how detrimental it is or how it can morph and escalate into other iterations. One of the most vital keys to understanding our anger and reacting redemptively to it is to expand our categories beyond the scope of its most heinous forms. As you saw in the Anger Spectrum, anger has more manifestations than you might imagine. If you did not see your most-oft-repeated anger manifestation on the graphic, include it while asking the Lord to help you do the heart work to mortify it.

Anger Diagrammed

> The saying is trustworthy and deserving of full acceptance, that Christ Jesus came into the world to save sinners, of whom I am the foremost. But I received mercy...
>
> (1 Timothy 1:15–16)

The core issue with anger is unbelief. The person does not trust God at the moment of tension to accomplish what they want, so they "believe in themselves" by using anger as a manipulative tool to achieve what the Lord would not do. Thus, sinful anger is motivated by a heart of fear that says, "I'm not going to get what I want," However, in this chapter, I want to pass on the heart-motivated fear problem for now and look at something else. Later in the book, I will discuss how our insecurities or fears of not getting something we crave tempt us to anger. In this chapter, I want to address a more critical heart motivation that entices a person to yield to anger's temptations.

That critical sinful heart motive is self-righteousness—a greater-than, better-than attitude of the heart. I will sometimes diagram their anger for them when working with people who struggle with anger. A picture is like sharing a thousand words with them. I have a sketch that I commonly draw for folks who struggle with sinful anger on the next page. This graphic illustrates Paul's thoughts about sin and grace when he wrote to Timothy in chapter one of the first letter. He wanted Timothy to know how he thought about himself, the foremost sinner (1 Timothy 1:15–16). Paul did not have a wallowing, worm theology but a biblio-centric one that lived in the reality of who he was before God lifted him from the mire of his worthlessness (Romans 3:10–12). Speaking of our pre-regenerative condition, if we do not perceive ourselves as the worst sinner in the room, it will be a quick step to don the greater-than-better-than mindset. The Bible's word for this deceptive condition is self-righteousness.

Anger Elevates

From Paul's perspective, no person was worse than how he viewed himself before he met Jesus on the Damascus Road. Paul saw himself as the foremost sinner who had received mercy from the Lord. That is, he was the worst of all sinners who received the grace of God (Ephesians 2:8–9). Those two realities—his sinfulness and God's grace—were core anchor points in his theology of sanctification. He was the most prominent sinner in the room regardless of who else was with him, a rational perspective when working through sinful anger problems. Without that view, we will succumb to anger's temptations by clinging to the false theology that says we are not the worst sinners we know.

As my grandmother used to say, "Ricky, do not forget where you came from." I appreciate her wisdom because we can sometimes forget where we came from, the grace that brought us to where we are, and how the distance between the two should continue to grow. If we lose sight of the past, which does not mean morbid introspection, the temptation to elevate ourselves above others will come quickly, especially with those who annoy us. This better-than, greater-than posture of the heart makes us easy prey for the allurements of anger as a way to put that unworthy person in their place, which is always a rung or two below us.

> *The Pharisee, standing by himself, prayed thus: "God, I thank you that I am not like other men, extortioners, unjust, adulterers, or even like this tax collector."*
>
> (Luke 18:11)

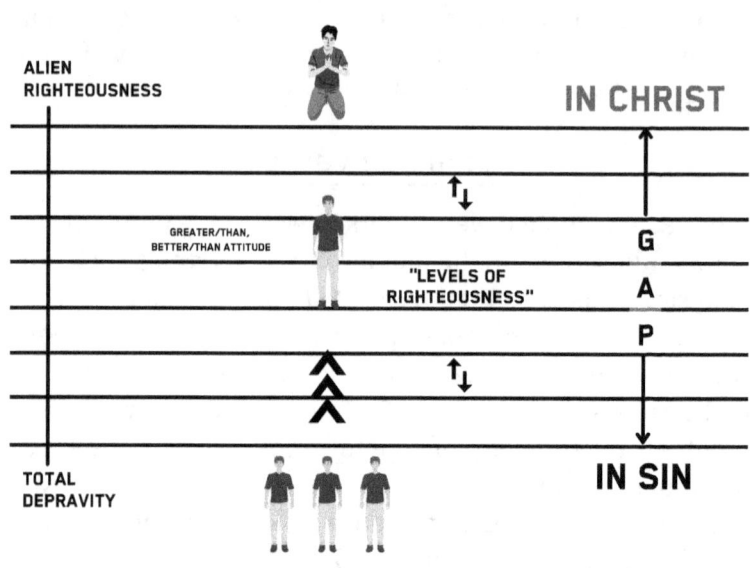

Anger Defies

> None is righteous, no, not one; no one understands; no one seeks for God. All have turned aside; together they have become worthless; no one does good, not even one.
>
> (Romans 3:10–12)

The problem with self-elevation is that no rational person can elevate themselves to superiority over another, at least not without mental gymnastics. As you intuit from the graphic, there should not be any degrees, gradations, or levels of righteousness among totally depraved people. There are only two levels: you're either in Christ or a "dirty, rotten, low-down sinner," as my grandmother would say. Self-righteousness is a spiritual problem that shuts out the soul from receiving the grace the Lord gives to the humble (James 4:6). The angry person defies grace by promoting his righteousness, which keeps him from grace because

Christ did not come for un-needy people like that—the self-generated righteous soul. He came for sinners, the lame, broken, and needy (Luke 5:32). The self-righteous man is clearly declaring that he does not need Christ's righteousness because he has his own. Here are eight sinfully laced quotes from the heart of the angry, self-righteous person (Luke 6:43–45).

- "I'm right; you're wrong" speaks to the righteous person's omniscience.
- "You're ridiculous."
- "You don't have a clue." Again, omniscience speaking.
- "You're an idiot."
- "When will you ever learn?"
- "Why can't you get it?"
- "I can't believe you did that."
- "You're such an embarrassment to me."

Anger Belittles

Then his master summoned him and said to him, "You wicked servant! I forgave you all that debt because you pleaded with me. And should not you have had mercy on your fellow servant, as I had mercy on you?"

(Matthew 18:32–33)

These self-righteous statements have one common theme: "I am better than you are." This attitude is full of gospel amnesia. This person had forgotten who he was before Christ saved him, assuming Christ did save him. He has yielded to the temptation to think he is somebody apart from Christ's work on his behalf. It's raw self-righteousness. On the other hand, an undeserving beggar understands his position before Christ. His sober self-assessment demotivates him from sinfully looking down on others. He does not forget where he came from. The unworthy beggar does not discriminate because he views himself as the pre-regenerate foremost sinner. How could he think otherwise? He was a beggar in need of grace, not someone who feels he deserves better while demanding from others through sinful, manipulative anger.

Anger's Gap

The self-righteous person has forgotten the gap: the distance between where he was before Christ lifted him out of his pit of sin (Psalm 40:2) to where he is now—seated with Christ in heavenly places (Ephesians 2:6). To live between those two anchor points is to appoint oneself righteous, an easy trap, which is the worldview of the Pharisees. Once we jump on the "I deserve better" train, we're not far from amped-up soul noise that creates relational tensions. The hard truth is that we don't deserve better. We deserve hell, and if we have something better by God's incredible mercy, we spend our days counting our blessings rather than making sinful demands on those we think are inferior to us. Take a look at a partial snapshot of the Pharisees' deplorable condition:

- They would not embrace the gospel as the means to righteousness.
- They forgot what Isaiah had told them about being filthy rags.
- They believed they deserved better, which they could self-generate.
- They made sinful demands of others as though they were different from them.

Anger's Attitude

Do not get caught in the gap between who you were outside of Christ and who you are with Christ. Everybody is the same outside of Christ—bad to the bone. No one is better than the next. You, me, the president, your pastor, Adolf Hitler, and Billy Graham are the same outside of Christ. There is none righteous. Only one thing makes any difference in us: God imposing His transformative gospel into our lives, which is the process of becoming like Christ. Outside of the unmerited gift of the gospel, even our works are rubbish (Philippians 3:8).

Paul never forgot this truth, which is why he could love and care for so many painful people (1 Corinthians 1:4). He did not create a man-centered gap between him and them. He owned the reality of who he was before God saved him and rejoiced in the undeserved mercy that God bestowed on him. For by grace, he was saved (Ephesians 2:8-9). That one truth will keep us thinking rightly and responding rightly to everyone in our lives. It will keep us humble, the one heart condition that sets us up to receive more grace (James 4:6).

Anger's Negativity

The culture teaches us that the pathway to success begins with having a proper self-estimation of ourselves, which always means thinking we're better than we are. Thus, when they hear "you are the biggest sinner in the room" as the pathway to success, they recoil and rage at such nonsensical teaching and say, "It's damaging to our self-esteem." Assuming you have been born again, you do not have to stay in the worst sinner category. You must continue along with Paul's thought progression: God has shown mercy to you (1 Timothy 1:16). You are no longer that person. You have been born from above (John 3:7; Romans 10:13).

Acknowledging the horribleness of your soul condition is not a sin-centered wallowing in the earthly mire for the forgiven soul. In one of his last letters, Paul reminded us at the end of his life that he was the worst sinner he knew. He never forgot where he came from as a sinner-man, even to the end. Our culture struggles with this notion. They promote thinking boastfully about themselves, demanding respect and rights at every turn. Paul had a comprehensive, self-aware, and honest view of himself that did not apologize for or disguise all he was, is, and will be.

Anger's Benefit

Your most effective positive mental attitude is never to forget that you were a worthless sinner (Romans 3:12) saved by the grace of God (Ephesians 2:8–9) and eternally secure in the hands of Jesus (John 10:28), who will always be for you (Romans 8:31) and will return to take you home with Him (John 14:1–3). Do you want to forget where you were, what happened to you, where you are, and where you're going? Remembering those four truths will give you the most positive mental attitude you could have while compelling you to walk in humility among your community as you give them the same hope and help that Christ gave you.

- Being too sin-centered leads to despair.
- Being too grace-centered leads to deception.
- Being gospel-centered leads to humility and personal and relational wholeness.

Anger's Defeat

Of course, being in Christ does not mean we have been entirely sanctified, practically speaking. Christ has given us definitive sanctification, meaning we have everything we need to grow into Him. The presence of and the perfection of our sanctification are two different things; we have work to do. Though the Lord has broken the power of sin and we do not have to sin, we continue to choose sin on occasion (1 John 1:7-10). None of us have transformed into sinless perfection, so it's essential never to forget where we were when God found us. It is not unhealthy or unwise to rehearse daily the fourfold comprehensive nature of the gospel:

- Unrighteous is what we were.
- Regenerated is what happened to us.
- In Christ is where we are today.
- Heaven is our future home.

Paul eagerly reminded himself of who he was before God regenerated him because he was also aware that he was guiltless before God (1 Corinthians 1:8-9). Sin had no power or persuasion over him (2 Corinthians 10:3-6; Romans 8:1). He had been set free (John 8:36). His freedom released him from thinking about his former life (Ephesians 4:22) and how he was in bondage to sin, one way that stirred humility and gratitude in his soul. The person bothered or managed by their past has not been set free from their past (Galatians 5:1). Paul experienced the neutralization of sin in his life to the point that it was not a big deal to talk about it (Philippians 3:1-12). It's analogous to moving from an apartment to a larger home. You rejoice as you remind yourself of where you used to live. The new homeowner is not sad about where he lived but is motivated to express gratitude because of where he is today. Our appreciation for God's "upgrade" should always be on the tip of our tongues, ready to amplify His goodness wherever we go.

Call to Action

Therefore I tell you, her sins, which are many, are forgiven—for she loved much. But he who is forgiven little, loves little.

(Luke 7:47)

Your love for Christ and others will be proportional to the width of your gap: the more extensive the gap, the greater your affection for others. The person who realizes the magnitude of his forgiveness loves much. Your temptation toward self-righteous anger will go away as you widen your gap.

1. Are you able to diagnose your heart as it pertains to sinful anger? Describe.
2. Talk about your level of gratitude for God's mercy to you.
3. Do you focus more on your sin, grace, or the gospel? Explain.
4. What are the dangers of too much focus on sin or grace—minimizing one over the other?
5. According to this chapter, what does it mean to be gospel-centered in your thought life?
6. How do you need to change, and will you share those things with a friend?

Diagramming Anger

3

Silent Treatment

As you saw on the Anger Spectrum, I have the silent treatment on the far right. Expressing anger through silence is an all-too-common communication conflict in too many relationships. The silent partner pretends the other person does not exist by ignoring them. Silent treatment sounds horrible enough, but if you place it within James's framework for anger, what we're talking about is, again, murder. Though consequentially not as bad as physical murder, it's a heinous sin nonetheless, which is worth a chapter in a book about anger.

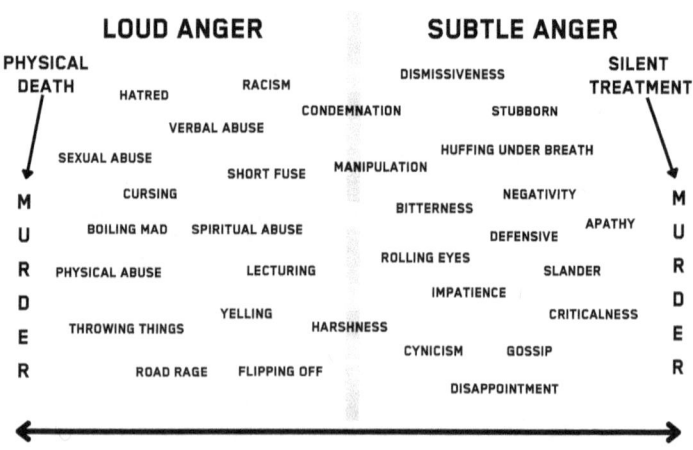

THE ANGER SPECTRUM
MANY MANIFESTATIONS OF ONE SIN

Where They Intersect

- Physical murder says, "I do not like you. Therefore, I am going to make sure you do not exist anymore; I'm going to kill you."
- Silent treatment says, "I do not like you, but I'm a civilized human so I'm not going to kill you. I'm going to pretend you do not exist by ignoring you for an indefinite, undetermined period."

Physical murder is severe, dramatic, and permanent as the perpetrator seeks to erase someone from this world. Nobody can be angrier than physically murdering another, but we know that anger is on a spectrum with one label for all its forms—murder. The two forms of anger intersect with the commentary they make about its victim: "I don't want you to exist." The silent treatment is a sanitized version of murder. If a person does not have clear biblical categories for their sin patterns, they can dull their conscience to the point of being okay with this behavior. A wrong view of the silent treatment permits them to accomplish a pragmatic result: the virtual erasure of another human being while dulling their conscience to make the "murderous" behavior acceptable. As they continue doing this, they will be blind to their blindness.

Slow to Judge

The silent treatment is not about an inability to communicate but a deliberate choice not to speak to someone. Of course, we want to be careful before judging the silent partner too harshly. Sometimes the person may not say anything because they feel inadequate when the communication becomes competitive. Other times, they live with a gaslighting, manipulative, over-the-top person. They do not sense they can speak in such a way to make a situation better, so they clam up. It's the wise path to the least resistance. I applaud them for not trying to go toe-to-toe with a communicative combatant. These folks living in this overpowering relationship need outside mediation and intervention. Their partner is such an accomplished jouster that they choose silence.

Thus, motivation for silence is not always as clear-cut as you think. You want to examine each situation with competence, courage, and compassion. Before judging the silent person uncharitably, you want to collect all the available data. Also, though there will probably be inequitableness in communication struggles, rarely in conflict is one person entirely innocent and the other fully guilty. While thinking through these things, one of our Mastermind Students—our all-online discipleship training program—came up with the following questions for the person who resorts to the silent treatment. The questions are in three categories: (1) motive, (2) Trinity, and (3) community. These question sets would be great for any interpersonal dispute, assuming both participants are mature enough to engage with humility. If working on them together is impossible, outside help could prove wise and transformative.

What is Your Motive?

I'm not suggesting that all silence is wrong, as mentioned earlier. James did say that being slow to speak is a good thing (James 1:19). There are times when biting our tongues is the best path forward for the short term. However, never saying anything forever is not God's plan for our relationships. God is a speaking God whose image bearers must emulate this attribute. Ask yourself these questions:

- What are you trying to achieve, accomplish, or prove with the silent treatment?
- What are you trying to protect yourself from by choosing silence? Is this a defensive tactic?

- What are you trying to control when you use the silent treatment?
- What are you afraid of by not engaging the person in conversation?
- What is it that makes you so angry? Carefully read James 4:1–10.
- What is wise about your silence? What is unwise?

Who is the Trinity?

Emulating the Trinity is one of our highest privileges (Ephesians 5:1). Hence, as you examine your motives, you want to align your heart and practice with who you want to represent by your speech patterns—the Father, Son, and Spirit. Perhaps there can be temporary justification for silence, but carefully address any log that may have lodged in your eye socket (Matthew 7:3–5). Today is an excellent day for corrective care if you need a spiritual eye exam.

- How does God treat you when you sin? (See John 3:16 and Romans 5:8.) This question points to any punitive motive for withholding your words from someone.
- Do you feel comfortable admitting your sins to God and others? (See 1 John 1:7–10.) If we know to do good, we don't want to treat God or others silently (James 4:17).
- Which is the more significant problem: your sin against God or what someone has done to you? The gospel has a ground-leveling effect on our souls. Though I would never justify any sin against you, I also know that whatever anyone has done to me is not worse than what I have done to the Savior.

Community

I have found benefit from reminding myself that I can do many things alone, but sanctification is not one of them.

There are too many one another passages in the New Testament for any of us to take the posture of isolating ourselves from the community. To live in a community is part of what it means to image the divine community—Father, Son, and Spirit. Reflect and respond to these questions as you think about these transformative truths:

- Are you aware of how sinful silence affects your family?
- Are there any other people in your life you treat this way?
- How does it make you feel when you are ignored and alienated?
- Does anyone hold you accountable for this sin if it is a sin pattern in your life?
- Will you change now? Will you stop doing this? What are your next steps?

Not that Bad

I trust these questions aid you in exploring your motives for choosing sinful silence in a problematic relationship. While the silent treatment may never come close to physical murder, it would be humble of us and helpful to others if we saw our anger the way James did (James 4:1-2). The temptation is to compare our sins with the sins of others. If we're serious about change, that attitude is not a redemptive way to think about ourselves. Perhaps if we saw our sin as the same as any other sin (James 2:10), we would be motivated to change. Maybe you're in a situation where speaking would cause more trouble than silence. If so, your relationship needs outside intervention. If you cannot talk to someone because of their anger, you need someone to speak for you. A pastor or other spiritual authority might be the best option. But do not choose silence whenever it is evident and proper to speak.

Call to Action

1. Define silent treatment.
2. When did you choose the silent treatment because it was the wisest approach at that moment in the relationship? What was the outcome, and was it wise to keep quiet?
3. When there is relational conflict, do you typically engage redemptively or punitively? How will you change to become a restorative communicator if you recognize some growth areas that need your scrutiny and improvement?
4. Do you have a gaslighting, manipulative relationship where you cannot speak? Who will you reach out to for help? What plan will you implement as you collaborate with a mentoring person?
5. When there is relational conflict, do you typically engage redemptively or punitively? In what ways will you change to become a restorative communicator if you recognize some growth areas that need your scrutiny and improvement?
6. Will you share your answers to all the questions in this chapter with a friend?

4

Seeing Clearly

Anger is a universal problem. Everybody does it. For many people, it's their most recurring sin pattern. It's easier to be harsh than kind, uncharitably judge than think the best, shut people down, and build them up. The first key to overcoming this habit for individuals who do not want to stay stuck in non-redemptive anger patterns is seeing themselves clearly. Like all our sinful patterns, if we don't see the log in our eyes, we'll never successfully work through any anger problems we may have. Our desire must be to have a correct biblical vision while we're doing the hard work of analyzing our anger.

Log or Speck

> Why do you see the speck that is in your brother's eye, but do not notice the log that is in your own eye? Or how can you say to your brother, "Let me take the speck out of your eye," when there is the log in your own eye? You hypocrite, first take the log out of your own eye, and then you will see clearly to take the speck out of your brother's eye.
>
> (Matthew 7:3–5)

James called anger a war within the soul (James 4:1–3). Thankfully, a Redeemer has the power to reverse the curse of our collective fallenness. Jesus also gave some helpful advice that cuts to the heart of anger—in His double-edged way, of course. The log and speck metaphor is beneficial as it provides a starting point while never ignoring the other person in the room. When I meet with couples for marriage counseling, I occasionally share with them Jesus' advice and then ask each partner, "Who has the log and who has the speck" in their marriage? Their answers are always instructive. I met with a couple planning to get married. I told them if they could correctly identify the log and speck persons in their relationship, they would have an amazingly wonderful marriage.

Of course, if they get the log and speck reversed, their marriage will fast-track to dysfunction. How about you? Think about your relationships. To jazz things up, pick the most challenging person in your life—that person who's a bit annoying. I hope it's not me. From your perspective, who has the log, and who has the speck? (Refer to Chapter Two: Diagramming Anger) When I asked the soon-to-be-married guy, he gave the correct answer. He said he's the one with the log in his eye—from his perspective. When I asked his soon-to-be-married bride, she gave the correct answer too. Praises. She disagreed with her boyfriend; the log was firmly planted in her eye; that was her starting point for conflict resolution. If their pre-marriage answers are post-marriage realities, they will experience a beautiful marriage.

Log, Speck Illustrated

> Then his master summoned him and said to him, "You wicked servant! I forgave you all that debt because you pleaded with me. And should not you have had mercy on your fellow servant, as I had mercy on you?"
>
> (Matthew 18:32–33)

- The speck person asks the log person, "Why aren't you angry with me? I hurt you; I've offended you; I've done you wrong."
- The log person responds, "I killed Christ. I put Him on the cross. Yes, you hurt me, but I can forgive you. I want to show similar mercy that Christ has shown to me. That's why I'm not sinfully angry with you. Your offense does not compare to my offense against God. With a log stuck in my eye, I know where I came from. All I can see from where I am sitting is the speck in your eye."

Like Paul, the log person never forgets where God found him. Though Paul did not wallow in or exalt his sin, his awareness of where he came from gave him a humble perspective toward others (1 Timothy 1:15), especially those annoying him (1 Corinthians 1:3-4). Paul's attitude toward others complimented the master in Jesus' story in Matthew 18. Paul knew his debt was massive, and God forgave him. If you're like Paul and not like the master's wicked servant, you see yourself correctly and will not punitively punish those who do not meet your convictions, standards, or preferences. Even if they need to change, you will engage them with a courageous charity with redemptive aims.

Psychology of Anger

Part of the war within that James talked about (James 4:1-3) is the complexity of interrelated fears, shame, and guilt that churns inside the angry person. The angry individual is a sad soul. They are reckless, but did you know this person is probably scared too? Most sinful anger is born out of insecurity, a deep-seated fear of not getting something precious to them. They fear not getting what they want, so they use anger as a manipulative means to satisfy their craving heart. This fear-centered reaction was the first twisted outpouring from Adam's heart shortly after he chose not to do things God's way (Genesis 3:6–12).

Once people move from trusting God to trusting themselves, they become a functional "god" over their lives. After deciding to do things their way, they walk away from the Lord as Adam did, which is a precarious posture for living well in God's world. Relying on ourselves rather than the Lord is not for the weakling; being the functional god over your life is hard. Have you ever tried being a god of your life—for a day, week, month, or year (2 Corinthians 1:8–9)? God did not build us to do His job. We cannot control all outcomes, so anger becomes a "go-to" tool in the arsenal of the weak individual who rejects God's rule over their life; it is a perverted power play to accomplish an unaccomplishable task.

Resistance is Futile

The habituated, angry person typically learns this self-centered worldview early. Perhaps as a child, they figured out how to manipulate their parents by using childish anger to bend the parents' will to fill a craving heart. Maybe the parents resisted, which was the child's cue to stiffen the resolve and double-down their effort. The child's unmet desire became a pouting demand, pivotal in the parent/child relationship. If the parents cave to the idolatrous demands, they will find it harder to resist their child in the future. This kind of parental capitulation to a child's will shapes the youngster into the functional god of their universe. Rather than orienting the heart toward the Lord, they set the child on the throne of his heart—and family. Their home becomes child-centered.

The kid's twisted mind and self-centered deductions convince him that he's the sole judge of how things ought to be. Somebody has to be "god," so his youthful arrogance and growing omniscience dupe him into believing he is the only one worthy of that mantle. Now, let's index forward twenty years: he's an adult. The angry person is a bigger version of the kid sitting on the floor throwing a tantrum, manipulating others to get what he wants. The same anger, born out of similar insecurity (fear), only amplified and more dangerous. His unbridled Adamic nature has now morphed into a habit, a way of life. He may be a Christian, but he brought his former manner of life into his Christian experience (Ephesians 4:22). Manipulative anger is a familiar friend that bulldozes a path, permitting him to access his desires.

Anger and Habits

There is a thin line between making demands out of episodic fear and making demands out of deeply-trenched habituations. A child not parented well will learn how to satiate his fears through anger. It will become his habituation if he continues down that path (Galatians 6:1-2). Looking back on his life, you will see how his habituated anger has worked for him. There will be a string of broken relationships his anger has carved up. "Gods" that parents help create will never be cooperating gods. Those so-called "gods" will devastate relationships and incarcerate souls. But there will be a twist of irony to this kind of sinful anger. He appears to be strong, large, and in charge. His bellowing convinces you of his power. The truth is that the angry person is weak, broken, and insecure.

To blow up at someone takes no strength. The angry person is a weak slave to habituated patterns of his making. It takes a lot of strength to submit yourself to the power of the Holy Spirit while walking under His influence and control (Galatians 5:22–23). The angry person never learns this lesson from the Spirit. Though he has human power (anger), he does not have that higher power (Spirit) that controls his human power. The book of Proverbs gives us insight into this lack of "spiritual power over our human power" problem.

Anger and Weakness

- "Whoever is slow to anger is better than the mighty, and he who rules his spirit than he who takes a city" (Proverbs 16:32).
- "Whoever is slow to anger has great understanding, but he who has a hasty temper exalts folly" (Proverbs 14:29).
- "A man of wrath stirs up strife, and one given to anger causes many transgression" (Proverbs 29:22).

The angry individual is weaker than they realize. The person who is slow to anger is submitting their human power to the strength of the Spirit (James 1:19). Fallen Adamic anger needs God's power to harness it. If it doesn't, it will pour over the dam of our hearts and hurt people. Let me illustrate: imagine the cap of a fire hydrant popping off. The cap is weaker than the force of the water. If the cap could withstand the pressure of the water, it would be stronger than the force of the water. In such a case, sinfully angry is to be without God—without a cap, which makes this person dangerous. Ultimately, the angry person shows a lack of submission to the Holy Spirit—the only One who can manage them while speaking peace into their heart.

To the Victim

> Make no friendship with a man given to anger, nor go with a wrathful man.
> (Proverbs 22:24)

Do not try to help the angry person by yourself. The person habituated in anger is not under the influence of the Spirit of God. They are without God—at least functionally—because

God opposes proud hearts; a warring army is arrayed against this person (James 4:6). It would be a fool's mission to go alone, trying to stop the angry person from being angry. They need a community of soul-care providers. The Bible's synonym in Proverbs 14:29 that describes the angry person is folly. The word folly represents the actions of the angry—they commit folly. The behavior of folly comes from the heart of a fool. By their fruit, you know them: their behaviors reveal their hearts—who they are.

Jesus taught us that words originate from the heart (Luke 6:43-45). If the words are folly, the heart is foolish, and the person is a fool. The angry person is a fool; you would be wise not to interact with them alone. Remember: this person is their functional god. They do not play by God's rules. You would be right to make your appeals, but if those requests fall on the hardened ground of an angry, foolish heart, you must talk to the spiritual authorities in your life, calling to them to help you (Matthew 18:15-17).

Angry Authorities

The angry person has limited authority over others, like in a marriage covenant or as a parent. It would be best to recognize that they have broken the first commandment (Exodus 20:3), which functionally disqualifies them from leading you. Suppose this person does not submit to God but functionally sets themselves up as a god. In that case, you cannot mindlessly follow fools (1 Corinthians 11:1). There is a mutual and reciprocal requirement for authority figures to lead and love those following them. If the authority over you is not leading or loving well, you must help them change, assuming you have the ability, context, and community to do so. The best way to accomplish this is by getting them help. It would be the height of unkindness to refrain from seeking to help a person like this—again, assuming you can.

The angry person is in a deep well from which they cannot extricate themselves. They can't lead anyone well if an angry heart has captured them. There must be a divine rescue; perhaps you and others can be God's means of grace to help them. Think about the wisdom of treating the angry person as though they had an addiction. It is a learned habit born from a fearful, craving, Adamic nature. The anger you see today did not just arrive in the angry person's heart. There was a trail of hurt and disappointment in their lives and unwise choices. The accumulative problems of the past germinate in the unguided and unmanaged heart to where anger becomes their habit. We want to do all we can to live in harmony with others, which might be your call to help the captured (Galatians 6:1-2). I'm not suggesting you can assist them, but maybe God will use you to be that means of repentance that only He can provide (2 Timothy 2:24-25). The angry individual is so elevated in his mind that he cannot see these entanglements of the heart. Christ is the only solution, but seeing the Savior is complicated from such a lofty perch (James 4:6).

Call to Action

1. Why does a person choose self-reliance over God-reliance? Describe a time when the temptation to rely on yourself through anger was intense.
2. What does it mean to submit your power to God's power? Why is this the wisest way to live a God-honoring life?
3. What are at least two shaping influences that might teach a child to manipulate others through anger?
4. How well do you see yourself? Do you perceive any sinfully angry reactions toward others? How would a close friend answer this question about you?
5. If you perceive sinful anger in your relationships, what is your plan to reconcile those offended souls within your sphere of offense?
6. Perhaps having a lengthy discussion about this chapter with a friend would prove wise. Will you talk to someone about what you have read and learned or the things that were helpful reminders?

Seeing Clearly

5

Angry Puppets

Angry people are like puppets on strings, always controlled by their cravings—something they believe they cannot get from others. (Of course, their anger is the tool they use to get what they crave.) James said it this way, "You desire and cannot have, so you murder." Mad puppets can't get what they want and react with manipulative anger. The cure for angry puppets comes when they see how their desires control them rather than God, and manipulating others to give them their cravings is futile and relationally suffocating. Let me illustrate with a case study about my old friends, Biff and Mable.

The Recurring Pattern

Biff's wife was late again. Her lapse was the second time she was late coming home from work. This week! She gets off at 5 p.m. and is usually home within an hour. On two occasions, it was after 7:30 before she arrived. As she walked through the door, Biff stood in the foyer demanding answers for her tardiness. Rather than asking questions to learn her perspective, he spewed accusations so she would know his viewpoint. Being omniscient relieves anyone from asking questions. Mable went on the defensive. The Christian lyrics in her earbuds turned to noise as her mind began to shut down. She did not anticipate his anger.

While there are many things wrong with this scenario,

I want to focus specifically on Biff's anger and how it had complete control over him. Every conflict is an opportunity for both people to change, and undoubtedly, Mable could do better, which is always the case with "less sinful" partners; we all can do better. Those on the receiving end still want to remember, "If possible, so far as it depends on you, live peaceably with all" (Romans 12:18). Paul's perspective to the Romans is my 50 percent verse. Paul says everyone is responsible for doing what "depends" on them. Mable needs to do her part, and Biff needs to do his. It's called marriage. Imagine a football field where both spouses meet at the fifty-yard line. That's what mature and humble people do. Good things will happen when both spouses are willing to meet in the middle, sharing, confessing, encouraging, owning, and maturing together. When one chooses not to do that, bad things happen. But in this chapter, the primary focus is on Biff. What can he do better? First, he can reacquaint himself with James 4:1–2).

Angry Puppets

Anger toward someone is submitting your thoughts, emotions, attitudes, and behaviors to that person. It's weird, I know—even ironic. Whenever an individual chooses sinful anger, they are, in effect, giving the other person control over them. They are like a marionette, a puppet on a string at the moment of their anger. It is not self-control but out of control (Galatians 5:22–23). The angry person is under the control of someone else, which is what happened to Biff. He was a controlled man: Mable owned him, though she did not know it, want it, or plan it.

Under the surface of Biff's heart was a craving for things he would like to control, but he can't—his passions are controlling him. In the battle scene with his wife, the underlying motives for Biff's behavior were the culprits. James called those motives passions, desires, and coveting—all synonyms that point to not-so-hidden idolatry simmering in his heart. Mable did not realize that she was Biff's functional god; she's like a soda machine that has what Biff craves. If Mable gives him what he wants, he will be happy. "Be on time," Biff bloviates. If she does not satisfy the cravings of his heart, he will use anger to manipulate his functional god (Mable) until he gets what he wants from her. She's his supplier, and he's the addict.

Suppliers and Addicts

The sad truth for Mable is that Biff could be married to Marge, Maggie, Mildred, or Madge; it would be the same problem. Knowing this is where Mable needs to guard her heart because she could say, "I'm just a Christian prostitute here to provide my addictive husband what he demands. He does not want me for who I am, an image bearer of God. He has one thing in view: the satisfaction of his lust-filled cravings." She's right, you know, which only intensifies the need for her to double down on guarding her heart, or both of them will be in the ditch.

Like all newly married people, Mable signed up for a love they hoped would conquer all their problems. Unfortunately, she married an addict whose primary interest is what he wants, when he wants it, how he wants it, and if he does not get it, he will use anger to rattle his god or soda machine—both synonyms for Mable—until she provides what he demands. Biff is so blind that he does not realize that manipulating others through anger is ineffective. But through many adverse shaping influences that predate their relationship, Biff is a habituated man, entrapped by these wicked desires that reduce his wife to an idol dispenser (Galatians 6:1–2). The latest flare-up illustrates this old and familiar pattern in his life.

Idols of the Heart

Of course, Mable was not thinking about the complexity of Biff's heart or the shaping influences that got him to where he is today. She was too busy shutting down, going on the defensive, and figuring out how to diffuse her angry husband. Fortunately, Mable is not a devious person who gets her jollies from playing her husband as a fool. She wants to learn about his inner insecurities that create and perpetuate his complexity. She hopes to wait until there are no "conflict times" so she can help Biff identify what has control of his heart and begin walking him through a process of repentance (Ephesians 4:22–24; 2 Timothy 2:24–25). He must understand that the problem is not primarily about Mable being late.

In one sense, her being late is a mercy from God that reveals something pre-existing in Biff's heart. His anger did not dramatically appear from thin air as though it was not already crouching at the door, waiting for a disappointing moment to pounce. I'm not suggesting Mable should overlook any patterns of tardiness, but Biff cannot tell the Lord that "she made me do it." The heart of the matter is that Biff wants something, so he chooses anger to get it. Here are a few possibilities of what might happen in Biff's heart that tempt him to get angry at his wife. This list is not exhaustive but a solid sampling to provoke you to reflect on potential motivations for anger.

- **RESPECT:** It could be he craves respect, and Mable was not "respecting" him by letting him know she was running late.
- **CONTROL:** He could crave control. Thus, he wants to know what Mable is doing at all times.
- **POWER:** His craving for control could tie into his desires for power or authority.
- **COMFORT:** Maybe Biff is discontented, so he blows up at Mable when he's unhappy with his life.

Need-Based Theology

The crux of the matter is that Biff has an elevated expectations (desires) and a plummeting disappointment each time Mable does not meet those expectations. He is a weak man. The real question could be: "Do you really need her to be home on time?" How many arguments have we gotten into with someone only to reflect and realize how silly it was? The angry person has too many needs, which happens when our desires morph into needs. Here are examples of real needs versus desires to see the differences:

- **NEED:** People dying of thirst will do almost anything to get a splattering of water to quench their thirst. The need for water controls them. They feel insecure (fearful), and rightly so, because they will eventually die without water. Biff does not need respect or total control of his wife or primary comfort from her—the way he demands these things. He must decide if he will love God and his wife more than these cravings (Matthew 22:36–40).
- **DESIRE:** When a child does not get his way, he may choose to pout as a tactic to get what he wants. He feels he "needs" something. This craving to get something turns to pouting (disguised anger), a tactic to acquire what he has elevated into a need.

In the case of the child, anger is a manipulative tactic to get his way. You know the irony: though he tries to control his mother, he is under her control. She is the supplier of the craving child, and if she withholds what he demands, he begins to feel he's under her power. The mother is like Mable; she does not see herself as the child's functional god but must perceive what is happening in this battle royal. If she does perceive the more profound complexity, she could begin shepherding his idolatrous heart so that he does not grow up to be Biff.

Power to the People

When Biff went off on Mable, he gave up his power to her. In the moment of his anger, she had all the power, which left her in a tough spot: to give in to his demands or ignore them were untenable options. There will be an impulsive reaction to give him what he wants; we're all like this. When those manipulating, pouting children become big and overbearing like Biff, their wives have lost nearly all ability to help them. If Biff does not repent of his sinful anger, he will keep her in that impossible place. Here's the untenable conundrum:

- If she gives in, she will feed his craving; he will continue his well-trodden, habitualized sinfulness.
- If she rebuffs him, she will fuel his anger, putting more strain on their marriage.

Of course, you have the added problem that it hardly matters what you do for the addict; he will never find satisfaction through "under the sun" methodologies (Ecclesiastes 1:3). If you give the addict his drug, he will demand more. If you cut off his supply, he will blow his stack. Mable is between a rock and a hard place, though long-term "addiction recovery" (repentance) is the solution, albeit challenging for any marriage in this type of triage. The vital thing to remember is that Christians have Christ, who is more significant than any sin, and that is our hope and help.

Call to Repentance

Under the spell of controlling cravings, fractured relationships perpetuate. At that moment, the only thing that satisfies Biff is for Mable to meet his expectations. It's a recipe for a joyless home as he has placed Mable in a position to be his god (Exodus 20:3). God does not bless willful sinners (James 4:6). Biff must begin the process of repentance to find God's illuminating, eye-cleansing favor so he can see clearly. He needs to (1) humble himself, (2) own his anger, (3) identify his heart idolatries, and (4) surround himself with courageous, compassionate, and competent helpers. Sin is irrational and disorienting to the person who is sinning. If Biff's sin continues to blind him, he may always believe Mable is doing something intentionally to tick him off. He may never see how his anger is inside him—as James said, not Mable or other things in his world. Biff's relationships with God and his wife are fractured. He must start the repentance process with the Lord, addressing his heart.

In Christ Alone

He must turn his heart from idolatry to hope in the God of all comfort. If he does this, he will be free from the bondage of fear, insecurity, unreasonable demands, and idolatry. Only Christ can satisfy his deepest longings. Because he has placed his hope in a fellow sinner—Mable, he shoots himself in the foot whenever he becomes angry with her. It's a setup for unrelenting frustration and fracturing of the family. Biff must wholeheartedly turn to Him, who can do far more abundantly than he could ever ask or think, according to the power at work within him, assuming Biff is a believer. He will have to decide if he wants to do the hard work of repenting, which is the only way to be free from the cravings that control him.

Mable's Addendum

1. As for Mable, she needs to reflect on these things, which will enable her to persevere in her broken marriage:
2. Pray to the God of all comfort. Live in His grace-empowered provision.
3. Practically pursuing God with all her heart. Despite her husband, the Lord can become her spiritual force, influence, and strength.
4. Guard her heart, especially about her desires for a better life or marriage.
5. Finding a great friend to help her keep her mind on the gospel track could be wisdom.
6. Additionally, find a community of friends to care for her.
7. Talk to her church leaders and enlist their help for herself and Biff.

6

The God Quest

All Christians bring parts of their past lives into their new salvation experience with God. If we do not see how we carry over these things from our pasts, we will continue accommodating our old habits, practices, and delusions (Ephesians 4:22). The consequences can be awful. The aim is to identify and break those old patterns that have always been with us so we can live a life for God and others. Let's bring Biff back out because we need to continue analyzing what is happening with him. Perhaps we can learn more about ourselves.

The Unmasked Man

Biff is an angry man. The situation with Mable is only one incident that lies on an ongoing continuum in their marriage. The oddity is that nobody from his church would know about his anger. They know him as a regular guy who loves God and others like the rest of the congregation. If you polled them, they would say so. Many of his church companions enjoy hanging with Biff. Of course, if you interviewed Biff's family, there would be a completely different story. Mable married Biff; she has seen him in the raw, no fig leaves. She knows the man behind the mask. Don't question their children, either.

Biff is outgoing, the life of the party, and fun to be around. Those who think they know Biff do not know him the way they should. Perhaps the church is partially at fault here, but you don't want to blame Biff's sin on them because they don't live with him. However, Mable does know him. She has felt the brunt of his former manner of life, particularly his anger, on more than one occasion. She and the kids know Biff as a pleasure seeker who carefully manages his reputation. Biff is a self-focused person. Life revolves around him. He has a misused, God-given strength that manipulates all things to a self-centered orientation. When things do not meet his expectations, he knows how to reorient his universe where everything (everyone) realigns. Regrettably, most of his Christian friends have not discerned this narcissistic pattern.

Biff's Two Worlds

Since becoming a Christian, Biff did stop smoking weed. Unwittingly, Christianity offered him a "cleaner kind of hedonism" where his passion for pleasure continues to grow under the radar and unabated. Though he loves God, he does not know how to live anything but a double life. The narcissism that has always been his identity had the rougher edges rounded by the sanitization of his new Christian life, which has never been difficult to disguise. Biff creates a carefully crafted representation of himself, explaining why his friends do not know these hidden secrets. They only meet Biff's representative in public spaces. Mable has met his representative, too. Not impressed. She lives with both the fake and real Biff. She "goes to church" with his representative, where they serve in ministry together, and she has to live with the real Biff at home while doing damage control for Biffy and Biffina, their two children. Biff is what you would call a living, breathing dichotomy: he is loved in the public arena while feared in the home. He is an unbelieving believer (Mark 9:24) who is unwilling to trust God with all his life. Though God has genuinely saved him, he does not work out his salvation with fear and trembling (Philippians 2:12–13), which raises the all-important question: what is Biff's core problem?

Two Worlds Colliding

Biff wants his life on his terms. When things go according to his wishes, he is an okay guy—in public and private; there are peace and harmony in Biff's two worlds. The bad news for Biff is that nobody can manipulate and package their lives according to all their preferences. I mean, they would have to be "god." Life rarely cooperates the way we want it, and it's in these "un-cooperating moments" of his life that Biff struggles the most. The uncooperativeness of life is antagonistic to the dream world where Biff is the self-appointed king, and everyone is complying with his edicts, and he is "living large" right smack in the middle of it all.

If only he could keep things contained, packaged, managed, controlled, and squished inside his preferred world. How great would it be to always be in control of all things? Of course, he would have to be God with all the accompanying "omni-attributes" to manage the vast expanse of his life. The bad news for Biff is that he is not God and cannot control his life according to his desires, dictates, and demands. We know this because when things tilt outside his ability to manage the situation, he unleashes his anger—the trusty manipulative weapon of the insecure person who feels out of control. Each time he unleashes his anger, his world snaps back upon its axis, and everyone falls in line.

Weight of the World

> Oh, taste and see that the LORD is good! Blessed is the man who takes refuge in him!
>
> (Psalm 34:8)

As you might imagine, this cyclic pattern of "in control, out of control, and using anger to get back in control" can wear on anyone, not just Mable, Biffy, and Biffina. Biff feels the adverse and overpowering effects of attempting to rule his world self-sufficiently. God never intended for any of us to assume that kind of dominion over our lives and relationships. We are to die to ourselves and live for others, not amplify ourselves to the point of dictatorial rulership. Biff must accept his anti-God worldview, including surrendering his desires to God.

He has lived in a self-gratifying, self-focused, all-about-me world all his life. After God regenerated him, Biff kept the parts of his past that he loved while tacking a genuine Christianity onto it, leaving him with a "suppressed hedonism." But it got worse for Biff. He married Mable and then had children, which brought more complications, i.e., more things to manage through manipulation. He wanted everything, e.g., selfishness, Christianity, wife, and children. Biff lives with a slow burn, but you would never know it because he only gets angry when he cannot get his way—a private sin that keeps his representative's reputation in tack, but if you disrupt his need for control, you will see the darker side of Biff.

Pressures of Being God

> All things are full of weariness; a man cannot utter it; the eye is not satisfied with seeing, nor the ear filled with hearing.
>
> (Ecclesiastes 1:8)

The weight of being "god of our world" is too much for anyone, which triggers the temptation to find an escape from the endless, self-reliant loop of our own making. When Biff becomes weary from running his universe, he takes a break by escaping to the temporary pleasure of his secret porn addiction. Porn is the "perfect medication" for a self-centered, self-gratifying, self-focused pleasure seeker like Biff, who cannot maintain tight-fisted control of his world. He can alleviate his frustration and general weariness from running his universe with a momentary escape into the "perfect drug" of self-gratification. Porn not only gives him an escape but permits him to stay in power; he can manage and manipulate the ladies of the Internet as he lives in the theater of his mind, where he can fictionalize anyone to do what he craves.

As you do the excavation work to get underneath all these things happening on the surface of his life, you will hit the most vital question that Biff must address: "What is wrong with God, Biff? Why are you choosing lesser gods, i.e., anger and porn, to satisfy an empty heart that only the Lord can fill?" Biff has a significant problem with the Lord because he consistently and relentlessly chooses himself as god over his life, picking his solutions rather than God's answers for broken souls. When there are only two choices before us, and we consistently choose our way over God's way, we're making a clear commentary about how we think about our selected choices and the solution we rejected.

An Unsatisfying God

> [Moses chose] to be mistreated with the people of God than to enjoy the fleeting pleasures of sin. He considered the reproach of Christ greater wealth than the treasures of Egypt.
> (Hebrews 11:25–26)

Something about the Lord is not satisfying to Biff, or perhaps there is something that he does not understand about God. Maybe his childhood was so horrible that he mapped his experience with his father over God the Father. Ultimately, Biff is not fully trusting God with his life, choosing to enjoy the fleeting pleasures of sin. He is refusing to trust God, and that issue needs sufficient exploration so he can repent. You will discover that his anger with God is part of Biff's problem. His anger is one of the milder forms, like "disappointment with God," which you see on the subtle side of the Anger Spectrum.

You cannot be angry, frustrated, or disappointed with the Lord and trust Him in all the ways you must have peace with Him. A father calling for a child to trust him will experience the child's reluctance if he is angry with his daddy. In addition to anger, you will also find "pockets of ignorance" in Biff's understanding and practice of who God is. Ignorance and anger are faith killers (Romans 10:17). Biff does not know God as he should. Hopefully, someone will confront, correct, and carefully disciple him to fully understand who God is so he can experience authentic joy. Biff has chosen the "lesser sublunary pleasures" of this world to satisfy him, which God never designed to bring contentment to restless hearts.

Living the Gospel

While Biff understands the gospel enough to become a Christian, he has not lived in the gospel's good after God regenerated him. A solid orthodoxy does not always equate to a practically proportional orthopraxy. He got his ticket to heaven punched, praise God, but Biff never learned how to live in the good of the gospel, post-salvation, practically speaking. It's like he came through the salvation door and sat down. By attending his local church meetings and participating in Bible studies, he has learned a lot of Bible information, but he is bereft when applying the Bible to his life.

If Biff is serious about change, he has a long road of hard work ahead. Suppose Biff follows this chapter's call to action and all the others. In that case, he will experience an actual transformation that will be measurable and affirmed by his grateful family. This process will also test his sincerity regarding transformation. Genuine repentance is not something he can manipulate—a nasty little habit Biff uses to control what he wants. If he is serious about change, the process below will not only bring it but authenticate his sincerity. But before I get into the call to action, would you take a moment to reflect on the Hebrew writer who instructs us about falling prey to immaturity? While reading about Biff and commiserating with Mable, we want to ensure that we're not following similar patterns.

Call to Action

You have become dull of hearing. For though by this time you ought to be teachers, you need someone to teach you again the basic principles of the oracles of God. You need milk, not solid food, for everyone who lives on milk is unskilled in the word of righteousness, since he is a child. But solid food is for the mature, for those who have their powers of discernment trained by constant practice to distinguish good from evil.

(Hebrews 5:11–14)

1. **LIVE THE GOSPEL:** Biff needs to understand the depth of what Christ did for him on the cross. This exercise is not a one-and-done pro tip for Biff to add to his knowledge base. Biff needs to surround himself with gospel companions. He needs gospel-centered books, music, and courageous friends in his life. He needs a robust prayer life addressing these deep-seated heart idolatries and gospel solutions. The glory, amazement, and beautiful truths of Calvary need to be his constant companions.

2. **MEMORIZE THE WORD:** Biff needs to begin a systematic memorization plan to allow the Word of God to wash over his soul. Christ cleanses us by His Word (John 17:17). Biff needs a severe cranial cleansing to where the motives of his heart and words of his mouth have a distinct Bible fluency (Ephesians 5:26).
3. **PRACTICE REPENTING:** Biff must understand what it means to repent. Repentance is the only means for removing sin in a person's life. Biff has been living in sin for so long that his conscience is dull. There is an at-the-moment repentance when you realize your sin and long-haul repentance that thoroughly removes those episodic moments. Biff needs to learn how to do both.
4. **BECOME A SERVANT:** Biff's life has been mostly about himself. He has not successfully modeled the gospel, which he can do by serving others. When Biff honestly comes to terms with what Christ did for him on the cross, he will experience brokenness by that cross. Once the gospel breaks him, his heart's desire will be less about what he can get and more about what he can give (Mark 10:45).

Never Move On

Biff must know that he should never move on from these four things. While there are other elements that he wants to deploy, he should never move on from these:

1. **GOSPEL:** Biff will celebrate the gospel throughout eternity. The gospel becomes his way of life.
2. **BIBLE:** Hiding God's Word in his heart should be a lifetime pursuit (Psalm 119:11).
3. **TRANSFORMING:** Repentance must be his constant friend—a constant cleansing friend.

4. **SERVING:** By becoming a servant, he will be as far as he can be from self-centeredness.

If Biff humbly submits to God, seeks help from the faith community, and does the hard things outlined here, he can break the chains gripping his heart.

The God Quest

7

Helping the Angry

Anger is a relationship-fracturing phenomenon that happens too often between individuals. The angry heart desires something from someone who does not provide it or is not responding quickly enough. Because their desire is not finding satiation, the craving soul angrily manipulates the other person. It is as though the angry person is saying, "I will only be content if you meet my need." In nearly all these cases, the short-tempered person has too many needs; they have taken their desires, simmered on them too long, and amplified them to what they interpret as genuine needs.

Primary Needs

Without being the word police, what if we took time to think about primary needs and secondary desires in the most technical and straight-laced way? Before you read further, it might be an excellent exercise to quickly list what you believe are genuine primary needs. Here is my list, and you will find only a few things that reach the high bar of actual life and death needs. I have placed them in two categories, physical and spiritual.

- Physical Needs: Food – Water – Air – Shelter (possibly Clothing)
- Spiritual Needs: Regeneration

Of course, secondary needs, like love, are essential, but only in a secondary sense. There are only six primary needs in the most technical sense. Love would not be of utmost importance if you were on a deserted island; you could live a long life without a reciprocating human love interest. If you were a Christian, you would survive more vibrantly because of the benefits of knowing and experiencing the love of God. That said, the problem for too many angry people is that they propel their secondary needs list to primary needs, which is why the temptation of anger assaults these enlarged, ravenous, needy souls.

Secondary Lovers

Desiring a good thing versus needing a good thing resides on different planes. It's not that you ignore the lower plane desires; image bearers should always reciprocate secondary desires to each other. Isn't love the second great command from our Lord (Matthew 22:39)? The transformative key here is that the lack of getting it from someone must not be all-controlling. The danger of elevating these lower matters, albeit significant, to primary matters is that you may become demanding or even manipulative if you do not receive them as though you were fighting for air or water. When secondary needs, desires, cravings, or lusts become primary, we will always live in relational disharmony when we demand others to give us these desires.

It also creates inequitableness in relationships. There will be the greater versus the lesser where the needy lesser makes demands of the presumed greater—their functional idol who is withholding the cherished desire. These captured needy souls have expanded their need categories that place undue anxiety on relationships as they exert power over those they can manipulate until they get what they demand. Most of the time, the needy, angry person has a low-grade fever that rides under the surface of their lives.

It is more subtle than the culture's rage, but it is powerful enough to rob them of the joy that Christ offers with the victory He won through the gospel. You will recognize them by their fruit. For example, here are a few illustrations of how expanded need categories place excessive demands on others while draining everyone around them:

- "Why didn't you pass the salad dressing when I asked for it?"
- "Why were you standing there so long talking? You knew I wanted to go!"
- "Mom, his bowl of ice cream is bigger than mine."
- "The reason I don't like you is that you are a critical person."
- "You never tell me you love me."

Love the Needy

> But I say to you who hear, "Love your enemies, do good to those who hate you, bless those who curse you, pray for those who abuse you."
>
> (Luke 6:27–28)

The question becomes, how do you help such a person? Well, you don't want to do what they do by reciprocating in kind, though choosing not to be angry at the angry manipulator does not mean the only option left is passivity. In Luke 6:27–49, Jesus decided not to get angry or become a doormat—two wise choices. You can be like Christ. Jesus was an aggressive, proactive man when responding to unlovable people, though His aggression differed from the angry image bearer who manipulates others to ascertain ungodly, self-centered desires. Sometimes His love looked like he was overlooking what was happening. Other times His love was corrective or confrontational, though never punitive.

Christ never did become sinfully angry (aggressive) or retreated out of fear (passive) when He did not get His way. (See Chapter One on the righteous anger of Christ.) Sinful aggressive, or passive behavior is not the way of Christ. The fundamental concept to remember is that if your worldview is others-centered, which Christ's was, you're in the proper position to respond well when dealing with angry people. Others-centered disappointment focuses on how to redeem the opportunity for God's fame. Self-centered disappointment bends God's fame into self-glorying contrivances that keep the angry heart preeminent and everyone else at bay through manipulative strategies.

Redeem the Needy

> God shows His love for us in that while we were still sinners, Christ died for us.
>
> (Romans 5:8)

Step one is to choose to love this person like Jesus. The "love is a choice" cliche is clever but a challenging maxim for living well in God's world, especially if you're the manipulated subject. Perhaps thinking about how God responded to you when you were difficult would calibrate and prepare your soul for the next challenging encounter with an angry person. For example, His transformative love was so powerful that you chose to follow Him for the rest of your life. You could say that He loved you into humble submission. The result of His affection for you changed your life forever—assuming you are regenerated. Alternately, Satan's anger from you complicates an already strained relationship by polarizing the fracture while pushing the other person farther from you and God.

Contrariwise, Christ's love pouring out of you inspires others to draw closer to you and God. The active, targeted, and specified kindness of God working through you leads people to a transformed life (Romans 2:4). You'll see this in mature Christians. They ask for little while their hearts are big with love as they enjoy the freedom found in the blessedness of nothingness. Immature, insecure, demanding people have a long list of primary needs, especially when people disappoint them. They only know how to get those desires met through manipulative anger. Don't be like them. They are not big but tiny people with foolish hearts. It takes a boatload of maturity to respond to this kind of adversity with the love of God.

Expanded Love

I am not suggesting you shouldn't confront an angry person. Paul did this as you read in both of the Corinthian letters. He did not withhold his confrontational, corrective care. You don't want such a narrow definition of love that it prohibits correction. We live in a snowflake world where you become a statistic of the cancel culture if you say something they deem unkind. For this reason, many people have volitionally chosen to self-censor. That is not love. We want to expand our love category to encompass all the possibilities, one of which is loving confrontations. The key to remember is that there is a way to do this, and we can do it horribly wrong. It would be well worth your time to read Paul's corrective letters to the Corinthians by spending as much time as you need with his preface (1 Corinthians 1:9).

> Paul, called by the will of God to be an apostle of Christ Jesus, and our brother Sosthenes, to the church of God that is in Corinth, to those sanctified in Christ Jesus, called to be saints together with all those who in every place call upon the name of our Lord Jesus Christ, both their Lord and ours: Grace to you and peace from God our Father and the Lord Jesus Christ. I give thanks to my God always for you

because of the grace of God that was given you in Christ Jesus, that in every way you were enriched in him in all speech and all knowledge—even as the testimony about Christ was confirmed among you—so that you are not lacking in any gift, as you wait for the revealing of our Lord Jesus Christ, who will sustain you to the end, guiltless in the day of our Lord Jesus Christ. God is faithful, by whom you were called into the fellowship of his Son, Jesus Christ our Lord.

(1 Corinthians 1:1-9)

It's stunning, right? Did you read the "faith for the process" that Paul had for them? He knows that what Christ started, He will complete. God will see it to the end (Philippians 1:6). Paul did not place his primary focus on what they were doing to him but on what God could do for them. He had faith for the process that they were in. Also, note his gratitude for them. If you contextualized what you just read in the environment and people to whom Paul was writing, it's mind-blowing that many Corinthians who read this letter despised Paul. Love is expansive, and the person confronting the angry person wants to choose the proper manifestation of love wisely while administering it with grace and truth.

One of the traps of the person who needs to confront another is the impulse to fire back with the "Jesus turned over the tables" mantra, their way of communicating their myopic and truncated view of love. The problem with this response is that it misses the target twice.

1. **ONE:** Love does include robust and corrective action, but love is more expansive, also including walking away, overlooking sin, encouraging the angry person, and examining the log in our eyes. If we have a narrow view of love that only confronts

and rebukes a fool, we will miss many redemptive moments when a different kind of courage is the best answer for the hyper-needy, angry soul.
2. **Two:** Yes, Jesus did turn over those tables. See Chapter One, where I talked about the three aspects of His expression of anger. Be as angry as you need to be as long as it's coming from a heart of humility, has redemptive elements, and those in earshot of your anger have a compelling desire to draw near to you.

Call to Action

As you make your way to the end of this book, this chapter is essential. While we want to understand the heart of the angry person, we also want the Lord to practically position us to be a transformative means of grace in His hands to help the captured soul. Will you take some time to think about how these questions might apply to you?

1. What about your need list? What did you put on yours? One of the traps to those helping angry people is that the helpers can have expanded needs. They have elevated good desires, "Why don't you love me as I want?" to primary needs. When this happens, two "needy" people are placing demands on each other. One must see their demands' errors and recalibrate their needs list to be a redemptive helper.
2. If you have an expanded need list, will you explain why you have them on the primary level? Will you talk to someone about how having more needs than the primary ones affect your relationships?
3. How do you typically respond when others don't meet your secondary needs list? Are you able to overlook it while mobilizing to help them? Or do

your needs and their needs butt heads? Explain your answers.
4. Keeping in the context of this chapter, what desires manage you? If they do, why do they? I'm not suggesting you should not have them, but what we believe we need will control us, and we don't want idols managing our lives. We need Jesus, and He should have primary management of our lives.
5. How do you need to change to help an angry friend change? Keep in mind the heart of Paul as he addressed the Corinthians. If you must confront, do so with charity, courage, grace, and truth.
6. After reading this chapter, what specific, detailed, and practical way can you change? Will you share these ideas with a friend? Who knows, they may realize growth areas in their lives, too.

Conclusion

God promised that our lives would be challenging because of the fall of Adam and Eve in the Garden of Eden (Genesis 3:17–19). All those who came from the first couple would struggle similarly (Romans 5:12). From the fall of humanity to the end of the earth as we know it, the promise of pain, suffering, difficulty, and personal problems is what it means to live in a fallen world as fallen creatures. It sounds gloomy because it is, but this dose of reality must be part of our worldview and baseline understanding if we want to live well in God's world while avoiding the temptation to anger when things do not go our way. Of course, Christians understand the linkage that though things are gloomy, there is glory, and it's ours through the finished work of Christ. We do not live as people with no hope.

Redeeming Pain

We're all under the curse of manifold suffering. From birth to death, the painful effect of the fall is ever-present. Even redemption through Christ does not immune us from personal problems. This reality is analogous to the omnipresence of the sun's heat. Though retreating to an air-conditioned room can be a respite from a hot summer day, that is not a solution that will ultimately protect us from what the sun can do to us. Summer heat and suffering are similar in that you can get a temporary break from either one, but you'll never be free from the daily rising of the heat or the recurring effects of suffering.

The conclusion is common sense: just as heat is part of God's plan (Genesis 1:3), so is suffering (1 Peter 2:21). The design of suffering is to mature us into Christlikeness, which is the redemptive purpose of pain, a blessing if we see it that way and act accordingly. You are aware of how heat brings life to the plant kingdom. Are you aware of how the Lord permits personal suffering to mature you? (Cf. 2 Corinthians 1:8-9, 4:7, and 12:7-10) Our kind and generous heavenly Father will permit—from time to time—unwelcome heat into our lives to protect us from ourselves. Yes, suffering has a self-protective element to it. Let me explain.

Humbling Effect

Suffering intends to generate humility that creates a unique dependency on the Lord that releases us as proactive ambassadors in His world. Suffering that we cannot change helps us recognize our inability to fix our problems, which is the humble heart's cue to see someone more able than us. Pain pushes us into the presence of the perfect One who can perform more powerfully than us. The wise person realizes their first impulse when suffering knocks is to let God answer the door.

Of course, fallenness is always crouching at that door, which instinctively tempts us not to turn to God when trouble comes. In those moments, it's vital to recognize that the problem is not about the heat but what it reveals about us. Rather than submitting like a soft heart that fosters humility, the heat in our lives can have an adverse, hardening effect. Thus, the rule of thumb is that "heat reveals" what is inside our hearts, so when trouble comes, you want first to diagnose what your problems reveal about you before focusing on the problem itself.

- What effects happen to you when the Lord brings heat into your life: hardening or softening? Think about two bowls, one with snow and the other full of mud. When the sun awakes in the morning, it will affect them differently—one will harden, and the other will soften. It's not about the sun, primarily, but about the constitution of the elements in the bowl. And so it is with our hearts.
- What is your pattern when trouble comes to you? How do your typical reactions to suffering events characterize you?
- You don't want to ignore any trouble, but you must not miss this critical diagnostic opportunity. What do problems typically reveal about the condition of your heart?

Cursing the Sun

I yielded to cursing the sun, figuratively speaking, a few times in my life when the heat came. Responding in those moments as I did, it's like a man standing on a mountain, cursing the literal sun because the heat was beating down on his head. Do you recognize any foolishness in that kind of behavior? My initial impulse was not to see it as God's active kindness in my life. Flailing away at the sun did not bring satisfying results to me or my relationships; it only intensified the problems and adversely affected all those in my vicinity, so says the sun curser.

The sun curser can no more change the sun than the angry person can create joy and peace by his sinful response to his circumstances. Perhaps discerning the difference between the sun curser and the humble heart will help. Check the descriptions that best fit you as you view the list below. This brief exercise could be a time to express gratitude to God for His empowering favor on you because of His great work in your life or an opportunity to work with Him to learn what you must change so you're not that sun curser. Carefully assess. Begin each line with, "When suffering comes,"

- The humble is mature. The sun curser is immature.
- The humble is perceptive. The sun curser is ignorant.
- The humble is grateful. The sun curser is discontented.
- The humble is wise. The sun curser is foolish.
- The humble is faith-filled. The sun curser is fearful.

Test Me

A vital question is why people respond differently to their situations. Why does one person curse the sun and the other perceive the Lord's restorative work through the heat stressors of life? (Cf. Genesis 50:20). Perhaps I can illustrate my answer this way. If you submerge a sponge in a pitcher of water and take it out and squeeze it, water will come out of the sponge. Why? There was water in the sponge. Rocket science, aye? When the Lord brings a negative situation into your life, take note of what comes out of your mouth (Luke 6:43–45). What comes out will give you an accurate assessment of the condition of your heart. There is hardly a better diagnosis you can take than to assess yourself when you do not get your way.

Those moments do not permit you to work from a prearranged script. They come instantaneously, and your instinct is to respond, and a quick response to heat reveals your most authentic self—for good or evil. Is your pattern to curse the sun when things become difficult, or is your pattern to perceive the Lord working in your life when things become difficult? Your normal responses to life's challenges reveal the quality of your relationship with the Lord (and with others), and sovereign God loves you so much that He will not refrain from bringing heat into your life to help you become more like His Son.

ONE FINAL PRO TIP: There is a good chance that even the problematic people in your life are instruments of righteousness in the Lord's hands to shape you into a vessel that makes you competent for use in His world. Don't quickly dismiss the heat that comes from those who irritate you. Who knows, maybe the good Lord is up to something you do not yet perceive but could prove to bring much fruit into your life because of His well-placed thorn. (See 2 Corinthians 12:1–10)

Call to Action

You have now completed my book on anger, but I appeal to you not to set it aside. Throughout this book, I have asked you many questions. If you have taken the time to reflect upon them, perhaps did some writing assignments, and even talked to God and others about your responses, you have already experienced changes. What if you go back through it? Let this book be a workbook that you use until your cooperative work with the Lord and close friends is so evident that people notice God's work in you. There are several ways to do this:

1. Write out all the questions from all the chapters, not just the call-to-action sections, but all of them.
2. Take as much time as you need to reflect and answer them. You're not in a race. You want to overcome any habituated anger patterns in your life. Be prayerful, proactive, and practical.
3. Share what you're learning with a trusted friend who will ask more questions. Your friend must be courageous and compassionate so they don't rubber-stamp you or speak harshly to you. A good friend will speak with grace and truth.
4. Find someone you can disciple or teach this material to a class. The teacher learns more than

the student, and if you can communicate these things, they will begin to "grow on you," even own you, and God will give you victory over anger. You will move from a self-centered, angry person to an others-centered disciple-maker.

About the Author

Rick Thomas launched the Life Over Coffee global training network in 2008 to bring hope and help for you and others by creating resources that spark conversations for transformation. His primary responsibilities are resource creation and leadership development, which he does through speaking, writing, podcasting, and educating. In 1990 he earned a BA in Theology and, in 1991, a BS in Education. In 1993, he received his ordination into Christian ministry, and in 2000, he graduated with an MA in Counseling from The Master's University. In 2006, he was recognized as a Fellow of the Association of Certified Biblical Counselors (ACBC).

Other Books Available from Life Over Coffee

Boasting in Weakness
Centering Your Marriage on Christ
Communication
Complete Marriage
Don't Apologize
Exchange the Truth for a Lie
Help My Marriage Has Grown Cold
Identity Crisis
Local Church
Loving Me
Mad
Marriage Devotion We Are One
Politics and Culture
Parenting Devotion from Zero to Adulthood
Sex, Temptation, and Modesty
Storm Hurler
The Cyber Effect
The Talk
Wives Leading
You Decide

www.ingramcontent.com/pod-product-compliance
Lightning Source LLC
Chambersburg PA
CBHW052150070526
44585CB00017B/2059